THE BUSINESS EMPIRE OF
CORNELIUS VANDERBILT

BY DENNIS FERTIG

Boston, Massachusetts
Chandler, Arizona
Glenview, Illinois
Upper Saddle River, New Jersey

Illustrations
2, 3, 4, 5, 12, 15 Tim Jones; 8 Joe LeMonnier.

Photographs
Every effort has been made to secure permission and provide appropriate credit for photographic material. The publisher deeply regrets any omission and pledges to correct errors called to its attention in subsequent editions.

Unless otherwise acknowledged, all photographs are the property of Pearson Education, Inc.

Photo locators denoted as follows: Top (T), Center (C), Bottom (B), Left (L), Right (R), Background (Bkgd)

Opener, Bain Collection, Prints & Photographs Division, LC-DIG-ggbain-50402/Library of Congress; 1 Bain Collection, Prints & Photographs Division, LC-DIG-ggbain-50402/Library of Congress; 6 Prints & Photographs Division, LC-USZC2-3436/Library of Congress; 7 Prints & Photographs Division, LC-DIG-pga-03828/Library of Congress; 9 Daguerreotypes Collection, Prints & Photographs Division, LC-USZC4-4160/Library of Congress; 10 FSA/OWI Collection, Prints & Photographs Division, LC-USF33- 012696-M4/Library of Congress; 11 Daguerreotypes Collection, Prints & Photographs Division, LC-USZC4-7421/Library of Congress; 13 Print & Photographs Division, LC-USZC2-2531/Library of Congress; 14 Stereograph Cards Collection, Prints & Photographs Division, LC-DIG-stereo-1s01729/Library of Congress.

Copyright © 2013 by Pearson Education, Inc., or its affiliates. All rights reserved. Printed in the United States of America. This publication is protected by copyright, and permission should be obtained from the publisher prior to any prohibited reproduction, storage in a retrieval system, or transmission in any form by any means, electronic, mechanical, photocopying, recording, or likewise. For information regarding permissions, write to Pearson Curriculum Rights & Permissions, One Lake Street, Upper Saddle River, New Jersey 07458.

Pearson® is a trademark, in the U.S. and/or in other countries, of Pearson Inc. or its affiliates.

ISBN-13: 978-0-328-67636-1
ISBN-10:   0-328-67636-5

6 7 8 9 V0FL 17 16 15 14

America's Transportation King

Cornelius Vanderbilt was a successful businessman. He moved far beyond his beginnings as the son of a farming family. Vanderbilt started with a $100 loan and ended up with a transportation business worth many millions of dollars.

In time, Vanderbilt became America's richest man. The country benefited from his power and wealth. The ship and railroad routes he created around the country helped the United States grow.

Cornelius Vanderbilt first used a ferry that had sails.

A Young Businessman

Vanderbilt was born in 1794 on New York's Staten Island. Today, it is part of New York City. However, then it was a community of small farms. It was separated from the city, on Manhattan Island, by miles of water.

Vanderbilt's father was a farmer and sailed across the bay to sell his products. Vanderbilt's mother made some of what he sold. She also managed the family's money. Sometimes she made loans like a bank. She hoped to make a **profit** when the money was paid back.

The young Vanderbilt was bigger and stronger than most other boys. By the time he was a teenager, he was bigger than most men. He wasn't afraid to use his fists when he needed to.

Vanderbilt learned to work hard. From his mother, Vanderbilt also learned how to manage money. When he was 16, his mother lent him $100. He bought a sailboat and started his own ferry business.

Vanderbilt's business quickly grew as he ferried goods to Manhattan. Vanderbilt was a tough **competitor** of the other ferry companies. He always found ways to get more business. At times that led to problems with other ferryboat owners.

As Vanderbilt earned money, he began to **invest** in other ferry companies. That meant he was part owner of those companies. When they earned money, he did, too.

The War of 1812 began soon after Vanderbilt started his business. New York City was suddenly filled with American troops. Despite his short time in business, Vanderbilt had developed a good reputation. As a result, the military decided to use his ferryboats. His boats carried soldiers and supplies all over New York City.

The busy harbor of New York City

A New Kind of Boat

In 1818, Vanderbilt sold his business. He wanted to work for another ferry company owner. Why? Vanderbilt's ferries were powered by wind. Thomas Gibbons's ferries were something new. They had engines powered by steam. Vanderbilt knew steamboats would soon replace sailboats.

Vanderbilt learned all about steamboats and also about business. Gibbons's company was fighting against another company in court. That company had a **monopoly**. It controlled all the steamboats that used New York harbors and rivers. The government of New York prevented competition. Gibbons didn't think that was fair. Neither did Vanderbilt.

One of Vanderbilt's steamboats

The Hudson River

Gibbons won the long struggle in the courts. In the meantime, Gibbons paid Vanderbilt well, and Vanderbilt saved well, too. In 1829, he had enough money to start a new company.

His new company used steamboats and stagecoaches. He moved people and cargo between New York City and Philadelphia. Another company also did this. However, Vanderbilt charged less money for the same trip. When the other company tried to cut costs, Vanderbilt outsmarted it. He cut costs as well. He kept his customers happy.

The other company realized it couldn't beat Vanderbilt. It offered to buy his company instead. Vanderbilt agreed. With the money from the sale, he started yet another company. This one operated steamboats on New York's Hudson River.

The Hudson River Route from New York City to Albany

As New York's population grew, so did the need for transportation. By now, Vanderbilt was well-known. For ten years, he did whatever it took to make his business a success. He bought one competitor. Later other competitors bought his company. They paid him a great deal of money for his Hudson River steamship company. They also made him promise not to run another steamship on the Hudson River for ten years!

A Millionaire

In 1834, Vanderbilt started another new steamship business. This one didn't travel on the Hudson River. Instead, it carried passengers along the Atlantic coast. Vanderbilt's boats traveled from New York to Massachusetts and Rhode Island. His ships were among the fastest and most comfortable in the world.

By 1846, Vanderbilt's business had helped make him a millionaire. At the time, it was almost unheard of for anyone to have that much money.

This photo of Vanderbilt was taken in 1845 when he was about fifty years old.

The Gold Rush

In 1848, gold was discovered in California. Suddenly, thousands of Americans wanted to travel west. However, California was far away. People had to rely on boats or covered wagons to get there.

Vanderbilt knew that the gold rush could make him even richer. Vanderbilt began to run steamships from New York City to California. Other companies' ships reached California by sailing around South America. Vanderbilt, however, had traveled into the Central American country of Nicaragua. He'd found a shortcut. His passengers traveled by a combination of boat and stagecoach to reach California. His trips were cheaper and faster.

People flocked to California to pan for gold.

San Francisco's harbor was crowded with boats.

Once again, competitors knew that Vanderbilt could beat them or cost them a great deal of money. Once again, they offered to buy his company. Vanderbilt sold once more, adding to his fortune.

Both Vanderbilt and his competitors helped people get to California. Most of those people didn't find gold. But many did earn money. They built successful businesses and cities in the new state of California. And, along with Vanderbilt, the country grew richer.

Railroads

In 1861, the United States was torn apart by the Civil War. By this time, Vanderbilt had steamboats that crossed the Atlantic. He let his fastest steamship be used by the Northern navy. Was Vanderbilt being generous? No, he had his eye on yet another method of transportation instead.

The different method was railroads. Railroads had been around since about 1830. As a younger man, Vanderbilt hadn't believed that railroads could make money. However, later, he began to change his mind. He started investing money in a company called the New York & Harlem Railroad. Soon he owned it.

Vanderbilt gave the North this ship to use during the Civil War.

This cartoon shows Vanderbilt, on the left, competing against another company to build railroad lines.

When Vanderbilt bought the railroad, it was in bad shape. However, he soon improved the company. Now, Vanderbilt started to build a railroad empire. He worked hard and used his tough methods to beat his competitors.

As Vanderbilt expanded his railroads, he improved the country's railroad system. The older railroad companies had short routes, odd schedules, and bad equipment. Vanderbilt's company had regular schedules and routes that traveled to more places. As he improved the railroads, Vanderbilt grew wealthier.

Grand Central Terminal provided jobs for people.

By 1873, Vanderbilt's railroads covered the northeastern part of the United States. The trains carried passengers and **resources** across the country. The empire included the first trains that ran from New York to Chicago.

In the late 1860s, Vanderbilt began building Grand Central Terminal in New York City. Trains from his railroad companies would end or begin their routes there. In 1873, hard times hit the American **economy**. Many people lost their jobs, and many businesses closed. But Vanderbilt kept thousands of people working on the terminal. The money they earned and spent kept things from getting even worse.

Remembering Vanderbilt

Vanderbilt died in 1877 at the age of 82. At the time of his death, his wealth was about $100 million. This likely made him the richest man in the country. Vanderbilt was a smart, tough businessman who believed that competition was good for business.

In Vanderbilt's lifetime, much had changed. America had gone from a country of mostly farmers to a country with many new industries. Vanderbilt's efforts gave the country new methods of transportation. His businesses changed America.

Glossary

competitor a company that is in the same kind of business as another company

economy the ways a country manages its resources to help people meet their wants and needs

invest to pay money into a business in the hope of making a profit

monopoly the complete control of a type of business

profit money made from a business or investment after expenses are paid

resource something used by a business to produce products